the Jesus

study series

All proceeds from this book go directly to the McKean Scholarship Foundation of MERCY*worldwide.* The McKean Scholarship Foundation was established in 2020 by Dr. Kip McKean in honor of his parents Admiral & Mrs. Thomas W. and Kim McKean. These funds are used exclusively to support educational opportunities for children in developing nations.

the Jesus study series

Cover Credit – Jake Studer

ISBN: 9798853077102

First Print – First Edition

TABLE OF CONTENTS

PREFACE

The following was my July 3, 2023 email to the Evangelists and Women's Ministry Leaders of South Asia. To give them a broader perspective, I shared the history of my building a study series to bring people to faith in Jesus Christ, and to thank them for helping me construct a new and more effective *Jesus Study Series* so that we can obey Jesus' Great Commission to ***"go and make disciples of all nations."*** (Matthew 28:18-20)

Dr. Kip McKean

Dear South Asia Leadership Family,

Good afternoon from Los Angeles! Praise God for yesterday's Bangkok International Christian Church Inaugural Service as 11 disciples had 67 in attendance! As well, Carl Basay a PhD Student from Chulalongkorn University (the #1 University in Thailand) – was baptized!

The Scripture in 1 Timothy 2:3-4 has guided me from my days as a young evangelist to date, ***"God our Savior wants all people to be saved and to come to a knowledge of the truth."*** This passage clearly teaches that it is the will of God for all men and women to be saved. After reading just these two verses, it is essential to ask oneself the question, "Is God's will, my will?" If it is, then you too believe in the evangelization of all nations in THIS generation.

In 1989, I felt the Lord calling Elena and me to lead the planting of the Bangkok Church of Christ (later renamed the Bangkok International Church of Christ). Since Thailand was a Buddhist nation, the Spirit put on my heart to build a set of studies to bring people to faith in Jesus before we would start the *First Principles Studies*. Therefore, to meet this glaring need in a faithless world, I composed the *Jesus Studies,* which were three studies widely used with several variations in the International Churches of Christ in the ensuing years.

This year on my heart was the desire to unify the teachings throughout the International Christian Churches (ICC) on helping the lost come to an unwavering faith in God with a deep conviction that Jesus is the Savior of the world. Therefore, I "dug up" my old *Jesus Studies,* and then I carefully examined Raja Rajan's four-part *Study Series* which included: "Does God Exist?" "Who Is God?" "Who Is Jesus? Part One," and "Who Is Jesus? Part Two." (I must admit it brought a smile to my face to see sections of my old *Jesus Studies* in Raja's series!) Since I have not worked for lengthy periods of time in India or Nepal, I really appreciated your insights and feedback on studying with Hindus, Muslims, and Atheists after you reviewed my "first pass" on this new series.

During the past month, I prayed to God to help me build a new *Jesus Study Series* to more effectively convert Atheists, Hindus, Muslims, Buddhists, Jews, Animists, etc. in all nations. (Afterall, of the eight billion people in the world, only one fourth claim any kind of faith in God and Jesus.) I wanted to create a simplistic set of studies that could be memorized. Thus, their purpose would be the same as my *First Principles Studies:* "To Solidify, Unify, and Multiply." My vision is to "equip" every disciple – not just the paid staff – to be able to study with their friends and families as well as to increase the number of fruitful leaders who can "study all the way through" bringing a person to faith, making them into a disciple, then baptizing them! This gives us multiplication!

As you are aware, Blady and Cielo Perez, the Bangkok ICC Church Leaders, are the Geographic Sector Leaders for "Indochina" which includes the Buddhist nations where we have International Christian Churches in Cambodia (97% Buddhist), Myanmar (88% Buddhist), Vietnam (45% Animists / 16% Buddhist), and of course newly planted Thailand (94% Buddhist)! This was Blady's and Cielo's response last week to my request for input from their almost three decades of ministry in Buddhist nations to build these "new" *Jesus Studies* that all of you so "patiently" helped me refine in New Delhi:

> *Greetings from the Land of Smiles! ...I read through your new Jesus Series Studies in my quiet time today and I'm blown away and inspired by how you comprehensively put it together. This Jesus Study Series is going to be*

super helpful in studying with Atheists and Buddhists! No need to add anything. Do you mind if I borrow some of your points to preach for this Sunday's Inaugural? Can we start using it now and probably start working on the Thai translation for the Bangkok ICC and the Khmer translation for the Phnom Penh ICC? Thanks so much dear brother…

So, on a go-forward basis, "we" too will now use the new *Jesus Study Series* in South Asia, as well as translate them into Hindi, Tamil, Bengali, and Nepalese. Indeed, around the world, we will preach the studies of "The Existence of God," "The Love of God," "Jesus Is God," and "Jesus Is Lord" ***"everywhere in every church."*** (1 Corinthians 4:17)

Again, thank you to Raja and to all of you for your discerning input... I learned so much! Missing you and I'll never forget our "Evening of Atonement" in New Delhi on Monday, June 19th followed the next night by that special Communion where we pledged before God, "We are family... to the end."

With all my admiration, appreciation, and affection,
Kip

STUDY #1
THE EXISTENCE OF GOD

Introduction: The purpose of this study is to bring atheists and agnostics to the conviction that God is very real and that the evidence is undeniable.

Romans 1:20 *"For since the creation of the world God's invisible qualities – His eternal power and divine nature – have been clearly seen, being understood from what has been made, so that people are without excuse."*

God has made Himself known through His power and divine nature evidenced in His creation. Science backs this up.

I. COSMOLOGY

Cosmology is the science of the origin and development of the universe.

If every effect must have an adequate cause, then there are only three explanations as to the cause of the universe: A) It is self-created; B) It has always existed and therefore is uncreated; C) It was created by a being other than itself.

A) Self-creation is unreasonable since a material object cannot "exist" and "not exist" at the same time.

B) Some cite the Big Bang Theory as the likely "first cause." This assumes matter existed to be distributed by the Bang. The widely accepted Law of the Conservation of Matter is that the amount of matter stays the same, even when matter changes form. Therefore, it is argued that in and of itself, matter cannot be created or destroyed. Consequently, the Big Bang Theory cannot be the "first cause."

C) Ultimately, matter must have come from another source... a Creator Being – God. In other words: God created something out of nothing.

D) Size of this magnitude implies a Being of unimaginable power.

God is the only cause adequate for such a vast universe. Consider the following scientific observations:

1. The Earth is a 6,000,000,000,000,000,000,000,000 (six quadrillion) kilograms sphere rotating in space.
2. Our sun – which is a star – has a diameter of 1.4 million kilometers – one hundred times that of Earth's – and could fit 1.3 million earths inside it.
3. The Milky Way is the galaxy that contains our Solar System. There are 200 billion stars in the Milky Way Galaxy. There are an estimated 2 trillion galaxies in the universe.
4. Scientists have estimated the distance from Earth to the edge of the universe is 47 billion light years. However, it is difficult to estimate how far the universe extends beyond what we can see since many believe the universe has been expanding outwards ever since its inception. Scientists believe the universe is 13.7 billion years old. Yet the size of it is unimaginably bigger than the speed of light, the fastest entity in existence. Obviously, something outside of and beyond space, time, and matter created the universe.

II. TELEOLOGY

The teleological proof of God's existence asserts that when an object reflects a purpose, goal, or design, it must have had a designer.

1. **Creator:** Analogy of iPhone found on a beach. Did millions of years of waves, sun, volcanic eruptions, time, and chance form this complex device? Conclusion: There must have been an intelligent creator. (For the sake of argument, the assumption is made that both Apple and Android phones have intelligent designers!)

2. **Order:** In science, the Periodic Table is used in Physics, Chemistry, and Biology with consensus by scientists. This simple chart arranges all the chemical elements known to man by their atomic number, electron configuration, and recurring chemical properties. In the basic form, the

118 elements are presented in order of increasing atomic number – the number of protons in the nucleus of the atom. Originally conceived by Dmitri Mendeleev in 1869, he rightfully predicted that there were elements with successive numbers of protons – 1, 2, 3, 4, etc. to 94. Therefore, he left gaps for those undiscovered elements which in over a century were eventually all discovered. Today, in the entire known universe, there are only 94 naturally occurring elements; the remaining 24 are man-made. Conclusion: With so exact but few building blocks to build the entire and ever-expanding universe, there must be one master creator.

3. **Solar System:** Again, we see a God of Order. The position of the sun and the way the nine planets are arranged is very precise. The distance of the Earth from the sun supports the perfect condition for human beings to exist. Had the Earth been a little farther away, it would have been too cold to support life. Had the Earth been a little closer, any life on this planet would have been burned beyond existence. These distances are too precisely calculated to be coincidental.

III. ANTHROPOLOGY

Anthropology is the study of man (anthropos) – his biological, physiological, and sociological characteristics – essentially, what makes us human.

Genesis 1:26-27 *"Then God said, 'Let us make mankind in our image, in our likeness, so that they may rule over the fish in the sea and the birds in the sky, over the livestock and all the wild animals, and over all the creatures that move along the ground.' So God created mankind in his own image, in the image of God he created them; male and female he created them."* Man is more than an intelligent being. He is the offspring of God, created in His image. Although animals are fascinating creatures also made by God, they do not desire to know God through worship and prayer. They do not self-reflect and self-adjust to a moral standard. Allen Webster relates humorously, "No dog lies awake at night thinking, *I should not have been so mean to that cat today. Tomorrow I am going to do better.*"

What do you think about the moral values that humans have? Kindness, joy, forgiveness, generosity, empathy, love are emotions that do not simply exist because you have space, time, mass, and energy – the four things that most atheists believe of which the universe is composed. Mass and time cannot develop love and care. Another example of man's created uniqueness is his conscious state of mind. The mere ability to question why, what, and when is unexplainable and absent in other living beings. Moral values were created by a sinless God.

Ecclesiastes 3:11 "He has made everything beautiful in its time. He has also set eternity in the human heart; yet no one can fathom what God has done from beginning to end." This verse posits that God has put eternity into mankind's hearts. Mankind wonders what will happen to them when they die, and they sense that there is life after death. The anthropological proof for God's existence states that if eternity and morality exist, then so too does God exist! He alone gives life, and he alone has the power over death.

IV. CONCLUSION

Cosmology, Teleology, and Anthropology – the evidence of *"God's eternal power and divine nature – having been clearly seen"* leave us *"without excuse"* but to believe in the existence of one true God. Do you believe that God is?

This "Existence of God Study" has borrowed and quoted from Raja Rajan's previously compiled study, "Does God Exist?" and Allen Webster's excellent article, "Three Arguments for the Existence of God."

STUDY #2
THE LOVE OF GOD*

Introduction: This study aims to bring atheists, agnostics, and non-believers in Jesus to the conviction that God is loving and desires to have a personal relationship with each person. The one God of the Bible is the Creator and is sinless.

I. **Acts 17:24-30** *"The God who made the world and everything in it is the Lord of heaven and earth and does not live in temples built by human hands. And he is not served by human hands, as if he needed anything. Rather, he himself gives everyone life and breath and everything else. From one man he made all the nations, that they should inhabit the whole earth; and he marked out their appointed times in history and the boundaries of their lands. God did this so that they would seek him and perhaps reach out for him and find him, though he is not far from any one of us. 'For in him we live and move and have our being.' As some of your own poets have said, 'We are his offspring.' Therefore since we are God's offspring, we should not think that the divine being is like gold or silver or stone – an image made by human design and skill. In the past God overlooked such ignorance, but now he commands all people everywhere to repent."*

    1) **Verse 24a** *"The God who made the world and everything in it is the Lord of heaven and earth…"*
- God created the world out of nothing.
- (This conviction should have been built in The Existence of God Study.)

2) Verse 24b *"…and does not live in temples built by human hands."*

- God does not live in temples.
- If God created the massive universe (or multiverse) he will not confine himself to small spaces such as temples, mosques, or church buildings.

3) Verse 25a *"And he is not served by human hands, as if he needed anything."*

- God does not need our services.
- God does not need our money, coconuts, milk, flowers, lighting candles, etc… He does not need our material offerings. He desires your heart and time.

4) Verse 25b *"Rather, he himself gives everyone life and breath and everything else."*

- God gave us life.
- One may say that his mother gave him birth, but it was God who gave them both life. If God gave you life, who should be our number one priority? It is not bad or wrong to be attached to your family, but the Giver of Life should be above them as first priority.

5) Verse 26 *"From one man he made all the nations, that they should inhabit the whole earth; and he marked out their appointed times in history and the boundaries of their lands."*

- God has marked out your boundaries.
- God has marked out your entire life. The year you would be born, your family, schooling, friends, everything. He allowed difficult times to come into your life so that you would feel a need for God. He planned out the little things in your life. That was considerable effort but that is how much he loves you.

6) **Verse 27** *"God did this so that they would seek him and perhaps reach out for him and find him, though he is not far from any one of us."*

- God wants you to seek him.
- God planned for you to meet "us" and for you to study the Word with "us."

7) **Verse 27b** *"...perhaps reach out for him and find him, though he is not far from any one of us."*

- God gives you a choice.
- The word "perhaps" shows that God has given you a choice on whether to have a relationship with him. Just as we chose our friends, God wants you to choose him as your best friend.

8) **Verse 28** *"'For in him we live and move and have our being.' As some of your own poets have said, 'We are his offspring.'"*

- We are God's children.
- Everyone born is a child of God regardless of their religious background including atheists.

9) **Verse 29** *"Therefore since we are God's offspring, we should not think that the divine being is like gold or silver or stone – an image made by human design and skill."*

- God is not made by man's design or skill.
- Is it possible to make one's own parents? Then what makes us think we can make a god, which in reality, is forming a lifeless idol.

10) **Verse 30** *"In the past God overlooked such ignorance, but now he commands all people everywhere to repent."*

- God is sinless and wants us to repent of our sins so we can have a relationship with him.

- The heart of God is love through forgiveness. In the past you did everything in ignorance. Yet now God has given you the chance to change your life. Take it!

II. **Psalm 119:1-2** *"Blessed are those whose ways are blameless, who walk according to the law of the Lord. Blessed are those who keep his statutes and seek him with all their heart."*

1) *"Blessed..."*
- Blessed means happy (superlatively happy).
- God loves us so much that he made us to be happy.

2) *"Blessed are those who keep his statutes and seek him with all their heart."*
- Happiness is not the goal of one who seeks God but the "by-product."
- To seek God, you must do it with all your heart.
- Seeking God means to "keep his statues."

III. **Matthew 6:25-33** *"Therefore I tell you, do not worry about your life, what you will eat or drink; or about your body, what you will wear. Is not life more than food, and the body more than clothes? Look at the birds of the air; they do not sow or reap or store away in barns, and yet your heavenly Father feeds them. Are you not much more valuable than they? Can any one of you by worrying add a single hour to your life? "And why do you worry about clothes? See how the flowers of the field grow. They do not labor or spin. Yet I tell you that not even Solomon in all his splendor was dressed like one of these. If that is how God clothes the grass of the field, which is here today and tomorrow is thrown into the fire, will he not much more clothe you—you of little faith? So do not worry, saying, 'What shall we eat?' or 'What shall we drink?' or 'What shall we wear?' For the pagans run after all these things, and your heavenly Father knows that you need them. But seek first his kingdom and his righteousness, and all these things will be given to you as well. Therefore do not worry about tomorrow, for tomorrow will worry about itself. Each day has enough trouble of its own."*

1) *"So do not worry…"*
   - If God takes care of the birds and grass, can he not take care of you?

2) *"But seek first his kingdom and his righteousness…"*
   - Your seeking God must take first priority in your life.

IV. **Acts 17:10-12** *"As soon as it was night, the believers sent Paul and Silas away to Berea. On arriving there, they went to the Jewish synagogue. Now the Berean Jews were of more noble character than those in Thessalonica, for they received the message with great eagerness and examined the Scriptures every day to see if what Paul said was true. As a result, many of them believed, as did also a number of prominent Greek women and many Greek men."*

   1) *"…more noble… for they received the message with great eagerness."*
   - Are you eager to study God's word?

   2) *"…examined the Scriptures every day…"*
   - Will you too study God's word daily?

V. **Jeremiah 29:11-13** *"For I know the plans I have for you," declares the Lord, "plans to prosper you and not to harm you, plans to give you hope and a future. Then you will call on me and come and pray to me, and I will listen to you. You will seek me and find me when you seek me with all your heart."*

   1) *"For I know the plans I have for you…"*
   - God loves you so much that he has an individual plan for your life.

   2) *"…plans to prosper you and not to harm you, plans to give you hope and a future."*
   - A plan to prosper you – with hope and a future.

   3) *"You will seek me and find me when you seek me with all your heart."*

- You will find God when you seek Him with all your heart.

Conclusion: Do you see how much God loves you and does that motivate you to seek him with all your heart by studying the Word of God?

*After finishing all four studies of *The Jesus Study Series*, "The Love of God Study" will allow you to skip the "Seeking God Study" in *First Principles* and start with "The Word of God Study."

STUDY #3
JESUS IS GOD

Introduction: This study introduces Jesus by showing how different he is from "other" gods and goddesses. So many from the secular world have a distorted view of Jesus. This study can be geared toward: 1) Hindus by comparing Jesus against Hindu gods; 2) Muslims by proving that Jesus is not simply a prophet; 3) Buddhists by helping them gain the understanding that Jesus is far superior to Buddha; 4) Atheists and Jews can see that Jesus was God in the flesh; and 5) "Christians" who have never read and studied the Bible.

In some nations, there is a widespread belief among people that everyone/everything is God. To refute this, bring in the characteristics of God saying everyone cannot be God and for anyone to be accepted as God, he should have these three exceptional qualities: 1) God created something out of nothing. 2) God is sinless and thus flawless. 3) God has power over death.

Colossians 2:9 *"For in Christ all the fullness of the Deity lives in bodily form…"* The Bible teaches that every quality of God is in Jesus. Jesus is the only person in any religion who has every quality of God. Jesus is all God and all man. God is not an impersonal tyrant ruling from above throwing lightning bolts at mankind, but a powerful God who cares deeply for his children.

1) POWER OVER DISEASE
Mark 1:40-42
Gurus, Pandits, and so-called Christian healers claim they can heal, yet they do not do so instantaneously like Jesus. They control the setting where they supposedly "cure." Only a true God can cure immediately and completely.

2) POWER TO FORGIVE SIN
Mark 2:1-7, 11-12

To prove he could forgive sin, Jesus heals a paralyzed man. Jesus is the only God who has the power to forgive, cleanse, and redeem you. Only a holy, sinless God can forgive your sins.

3) POWER OVER NATURE
Mark 4:35-41

Jesus controlled the wind and the waves – nature. Man designed computers therefore he is in control of them. Jesus controlled the wind and water as he was the Creator of the Universe. For Hindus, make it clear that we do not worship nature. For Muslims, in the Quran, Mohammad did not perform miracles, but Jesus did.

4) POWER OVER DEMONS
Mark 5:1-13

Many Hindu families live in fear of demons and evil spirits. Jesus drove the evil spirits away from the man. Jesus has power over everything even Satan, so there is no need to fear.

5) POWER OVER DEATH
Mark 5:21-24, 35-43

Jesus heals the dead girl. Only God has the power over life and death.

6) POWER TO CREATE SOMETHING OUT OF NOTHING
Mark 6:34-44

There was not enough bread and fish, so Jesus "creates" an abundance from "two fish and five loaves of bread" to feed and satisfy 5,000 men as he is the Creator of all.

Conclusion: No other person who has ever lived has had or claimed to have the power over disease, sin, nature, demons, death, and the ability to create something out of nothing. Do you believe? Tap into this power and believe!

STUDY #4
JESUS IS LORD

The Book of John was written so that people would come to believe in Jesus. *"Jesus performed many other signs in the presence of his disciples, which are not recorded in this book. But these are written that you may believe that Jesus is the Messiah, the Son of God, and that by believing you may have life in his name."* (John 20:30-31) This is a must study for everyone including those with a "Christian background" that live outside highly-developed "Christian countries." Throughout the world, most of those that call themselves "Christians" do not attend church. In fact, a very few do go to church, but often these few not only worship Jesus but other gods as well by celebrating Diwali, Holi, Durga Puja, and Vesak.

1) JESUS IS GOD IN THE FLESH
John 1:1-3, 14-18

- Jesus has always existed. He came to earth to reveal what God is really like, *"Full of grace and truth."*

2) JESUS GIVES A NEW START
John 3:1-5

- In speaking to a member of the Jewish ruling council, Jesus tells him he must be born again. You can start your life all over again with God.

3) JESUS IS THE SAVIOR OF THE WORLD
John 3:16-18

- God sent Jesus to save the world. Jesus is not only the God of all Christians, but he is the God for the whole world. He wants all men and all women from all backgrounds, all castes, all social standings, all races, all nations, and all religions to be saved.

4) JESUS KNOWS YOUR CONDITION

John 5:3-8

- Many knew this man's condition. Jesus knew it better than the man. Jesus knows your condition. Your boss, parents, siblings, and friends may not know, but only Jesus can change it. Do you want to get well?

5) JESUS GIVES A FULL LIFE
John 10:7-10

- For many life is unfulfilled and empty. Some have even contemplated suicide to rid themselves of their pain and apathy. Jesus wants to give you a life and a purpose.

6) JESUS HAS OVERCOME DEATH
John 19:16-18, 28-30; 20:24-29

Though Jesus died a horrible death by crucifixion, God raised him from the dead to prove he was the Son of God. Not only did the Apostles all see and believe in Jesus, but Paul writes in I Corinthian 15:3-8 that, Jesus appeared to more than 500 people.

7) JESUS IS THE ONLY WAY TO GOD
John 14:1-6

- God has prepared a place in heaven for us. The only way to God to be with him for eternity is through Jesus.

Conclusion: Ask them "Who do you think Jesus is?" There are only 4 possibilities of who he was:

- **Jesus is a lunatic** – "He is crazy! He only thought he was the Son of God." He spoke with such wisdom that so many of his teachings are quoted to this day. Many people tried to trap him in his words or find a fault in his life, but they were unable. Jesus changed so many lives – can a lunatic do that?
- **Jesus is a legend** – "He did some good things, but the stories grew bigger and bigger over the centuries." Yet the four Books in the Bible on Jesus' life – Matthew, Mark, Luke, and John – are eye-witness accounts. Matthew, Mark, and John walked with Jesus. Luke wrote about his account, ***"Many have undertaken to draw up an account of the things that have been***

fulfilled among us, just as they were handed down to us by those who from the first were eyewitnesses and servants of the word. With this in mind, since I myself have carefully investigated everything from the beginning, I too decided to write an orderly account for you, most excellent Theophilus, so that you may know the certainty of the things you have been taught." (Luke 1:1-4)

- **Jesus is a liar** – "He was deceiving the people about who he really was." People do not die for a lie. The Apostles were afraid of persecution and death at Jesus' arrest and so ran away. However, just 50 days later, in Acts 2, they were strong and uncompromising. Why? They believed Jesus was the Son of God resurrected from the dead. In Acts 4, Peter and John are arrested. Then they are brought before the Jewish Leadership, *They had Peter and John brought before them and began to question them: "By what power or what name did you do this?" Then Peter, filled with the Holy Spirit, said to them: "Rulers and elders of the people! If we are being called to account today for an act of kindness shown to a man who was lame and are being asked how he was healed, then know this, you and all the people of Israel: It is by the name of Jesus Christ of Nazareth, whom you crucified but whom God raised from the dead, that this man stands before you healed. Jesus is 'the stone you builders rejected, which has become the cornerstone.' Salvation is found in no one else, for there is no other name under heaven given to mankind by which we must be saved." When they saw the courage of Peter and John and realized that they were unschooled, ordinary men, they were astonished and they took note that these men had been with Jesus.*

History records that 10 of the 11 faithful Apostles were killed because of their preaching. The one not martyred was sentenced to prison on an island for the rest of his life. None of them ever changed their conviction – they saw Jesus raised from the dead and so no longer feared death themselves.

- **Jesus is Lord** – He is not a lunatic, not a legend, not a liar. He must be who he said he was – Lord! Son of God!

What do you think? I want to give you the same challenge Jesus gave Thomas: *"Stop doubting and believe!"* Then you like Thomas can say, *"My Lord and my God!"* (John 20:28)

Made in the USA
Las Vegas, NV
08 January 2024

83912239R00015